The 44 Laws of Peace

Peace

(And a few extra).

The Talking Book — Worthwhile Ideas

'So you're giving me advice, are you?' you say. 'Have you already given yourself advice, then? Have you already put yourself straight? Is that how you come to have time for reforming other people?' No, I'm not shameless as to set about treating people when I am sick myself. I'm talking to you as if I was laying in the same hospital ward, about the illness we are both suffering from, and passing on some remedies.

- Lucius Annaeus Seneca

The 44 Laws of Peace

Law 1:

Be present

The present moment is where life takes place. The past cannot be changed and the future is not guaranteed. It's a mere fragment of time in which we really live and it's this fraction of time that any of us stand to lose. Every time you distract yourself with anxious thoughts of the past or future you give up the present. This would be forgivable if you had power over the past or the future, but you don't, regardless of how much you cry. The only moment of time you have any control over is right now. Work to understand this and you will be more careful with how you spend your time.

Don't be like those that give up the present to anxiously rehearse social situations that may never take place, don't spend your time berating yourself over a past mistake, and don't get carried away longing for pleasant moments that are no more—for how can you make any new ones if your head is stuck in the past. Many are not aware that there is another way to live. They think these anxieties are as apart of them as the fingers on their hand. So instead of looking for a solution, they look for a distraction. Never spending time in their own company, they go to bed listening to anything but their thoughts and any moment of down time is stolen by the consumption of media. Anything to distract from the mind, so as long as they can escape their thoughts.

Know that these distractions offer only momentary relief but that true peace can be found by living in the present—even when the present is boring. The person who is thinking about nothing but the cleanliness of his teeth when he is brushing his teeth is at peace. He is living completely in the moment, his thoughts are directed towards that which he can control, and his mind is not held captive by anxious thoughts which are useless in the moment. The same goes for the man who doesn't let his mind wander when speaking with friends or family, but instead lends his attention to those right in front of him—he is truly living. Appreciate the now, for it becomes the memories you look back on so fondly.

Living in the present is an important step in calming the mind. So make the effort to be deeply involved with the current moment, whatever task may be at hand. When you catch yourself drifting from the present, obsessing in thought over the past or future, bring yourself back to what's in front of you. This will be difficult, but it will become easier the more you practice. The entire future lies in uncertainty: live immediately!

Law 2:

Strive to understand, not debate

Debate can be a healthy activity *if* you are engaging with someone who is open to reflecting on ideas with which they disagree. Unfortunately, most people are uncomfortable being challenged and, despite the best of logic, tighten their grip on their beliefs when threatened. This type behavior makes for a useless interaction, a lot of talking and no listening. Instead, work to understand where the person is coming from—especially if it is a friend or family member.

For some, it's hard to listen to someone they disagree with without trying to convince that person of their own opinion—they must let you know that they are right and you are wrong, because otherwise it's a thankless way of engaging in conversations, no "gotcha's" or "I told you so's" to feed their ego. And so tiny disagreements turn into huge arguments that could have been avoided if just one person worked to understand the other.

There is no need to debate over every disagreement. Pick your battles wisely. Most disagreements are over trivial matters that you don't need to fight to the death over. Instead of convincing someone that they're wrong, work to understand their thought process. Suspend your bias and try to see things from the other person's reasoning. Besides, if you are confident in your own reasoning, than there is no need to feel threatened when disagreed with—in fact, it presents an opportunity to test and strengthen your logic.

Understand—if your goal is to convince someone of your position, you've already lost because most can't be convinced they're wrong. Your goal, then, should be to understand their position. I mean, can you even be sure they're wrong without first understanding their reasoning? Go a step further and come together where you connect, and you will have won two times over: first, in better understanding your friend and second, in keeping your sanity. Realize, too, that we are all guilty of being hard headed at one time or another. Think about this the next time you're in a disagreement with someone. It's possible that you're the one being hard headed.

Law 3:

Listen to listen

If you want to create a better relationship with people, the most important thing you can do is learn how to listen. Most of us don't do it enough or have a warped idea of what defines healthy listening. Healthy listening is not dependent on your ability to respond with a comment related to the conversation or to bring up a similar situation you've experienced in hopes of relating to the person. There is a time and place for creating such connections, but hold off on it for now.

The true goal should be listening for the sake of listening, not to test your ability to create responses that fit the conversation, which can snowball into a person who listens for the sake of responding. Who hasn't been guilty of this? You want the other person to know that you're interested in what they have to say, and so you latch onto the first portion of the conversation that you feel you have something to say about and neglect the rest as you wait for your chance to "prove yourself." Even worse than this, there are many who enjoy hearing the sound of their own voice and will use any opportunity to take over the conversation--don't be that person. Remember, genuine responses come from genuinely listening.

Law 4:

Say Less

Do not over-explain yourself. People tend to go into long rants when explaining themselves and often spit out more than is necessary. Most of the time, these explanations call for no more than a simple answer: Late for work? Then tell your boss, "sorry, running late this morning." Rambling on about everything that went wrong that led to you being late is unnecessary. There is no need to go into a long, convoluted explanation unless asked. Keep this in mind, especially in business environments where over-explaining can come off as insecure ramblings.

Remember, the less you say, the less you have to worry about saying something stupid.

Law 5:

Commit to yourself

Imagine the kind of person you would be if you did everything you said you were going to do: "This week I am going to start eating better," "I am going to start working out again," "I am going to work on that side business I have been thinking about," "I am going to be patient with those that annoy me." Now realize that the only thing stopping you from being that person is yourself. To be the best version of yourself is as simple as keeping the promises you make to yourself. Unfortunately, like most things in life, this is easier said than done.

When we make a promise to ourselves we are eager to keep it and swear on our lives that we will, but when the time comes to keep that promise, the version of us that was so committed is no where to be found. Instead, in their place, we find a version of ourselves that argues like a lawyer in the opposite direction, trying to rationalize why we shouldn't fulfill said promise: "it's too hot," "I'm too tired," "that was a stupid idea," "it's not that important," "I can do it later."

You see, the reason it's easy to make the promise is because you are not the one who needs to keep the commitment, it's the "future you" who is responsible for that. This is the appeal of procrastination, it gives you today by promising you'll do what's necessary tomorrow. There is a whole sub-culture that grew up waiting to the last minute to complete a three-month book report the night before it was due. While not ideal, this mindset might work for school and work, but it is ineffective when it comes to bettering ourselves. There is no "due date." No one but ourselves to hold us responsible for our commitments to ourselves. That "future you" will be the same uncommitted you, unless you do something about it and change immediately.

Realize, too, that the more you break promises to yourself, the easier it gets to do so and the less you end up trusting yourself (whether you realize it or not). Breaking commitments to yourself weakens the will and conditions the soul to not take yourself seriously. It's the same when anyone repeatedly breaks promises: you become untrusting and take it for fact that they will break their next promise long before they are given the chance. The upside to someone breaking a promise to you is that it's their character that is at stake, not yours. However, when you break a promise to yourself, it's much more than your character that's at stake, it's your life.

It is possible to break out of this unhealthy relationship with yourself, all it will cost is a small portion of your comfort. The solution is two-fold:

1. Strengthen your will by making and upholding small promises to yourself that you can follow through with immediately. This can come in the form of making your bed each day, ending showers with the water on cold, keeping your room in order, taking out the trash when its full. These tasks should take no longer than 5-minutes, making them achievable for everyone. They are easily manageable to the point that to argue against them is silly.

2. If you can do something immediately, don't promise yourself you'll do it later, do it now. With little things, for example — don't promise you'll start working out tomorrow or next week, start today; don't promise yourself you'll stop eating junk food tomorrow, start today; don't promise that you'll start living for yourself next year, start today. There is no need to wait— that's just an excuse not to start, an excuse to push responsibility on a you that doesn't exist yet. Even the biggest promises can be broken down into manageable portions that you can work on today.

As small as these steps are, they will be the foundation on which you build trust for yourself. You have to feel comfortable walking before you can feel confident running.

Law 6:

Be mindful of your thoughts

Do not constantly disparage yourself or repeat negative thoughts to excess, doing so is a sure way to manifest those thoughts into reality. For as you think, so you become. If you think you're a good-for-nothing, you'll act like a good-for-nothing, and you'll treat yourself like a good-for-nothing, and eventually you'll be good for nothing. The same is true in the opposite direction—think you're capable of living a good life, you will act capable of living a good life, and soon you will live a good life.

Law 7:

Strive to understand yourself

Study your emotions, actions, and reactions to events. Most people can identify what makes them sad, angry, or annoyed, but few have devoted time to understanding why that specific thing makes them feel that way. People who go their entire life without examining themselves will find it hard to improve. For it is impossible to fix a thing without first determining it needs repair.

Law 8:

Discipline is the key to freedom

You would be unstoppable if, in the face of temptation, laziness, and impulse, you held true to the path you set for yourself when you were free from such distractions. The only thing keeping you from becoming that person, a person you can be proud of, is discipline. Work to strengthen your will. Work towards keeping your promises to yourself. At the very least, work towards recognizing when you break promises to yourself and others. The world is yours for the taking, but how can you expect to achieve anything of worth if you can't even conquer yourself?

Law 9:

Don't be an "all talk"

Just as important as keeping promises to yourself, is working to keep every promise you make in general and learning not to make promises you can't keep or are unsure you can keep. Don't feel that you have some social obligation to promise your time to everyone and anyone who asks, even if they are a loved one. This doesn't mean that you can't offer your help to someone, but before making the commitment of a promise, make sure it's something you're willing to keep, even if you don't feel up to it when the day comes. It's better to say no than to offer a false promise. Otherwise, you will become someone who is all talk and no action. Talk is cheap, you should be better than that.

Law 10:

Meditate

Don't neglect the mind. We are quick to go on a diet after eating poorly or to work out when we notice a change in our physical ability, but how many treat the mind with the same care? Just as stretching ensures a better state of being for the body's overall health, meditating provides similar benefits to the mind. Anxiety, anger, frustration, depression, and every other mental state of being, including the unending chattering of thoughts, can be made quiet through meditation. Most people are unaware of this and instead attempt to distract their mind with the consumption of media. However, distracting your mind with a flood of stimuli will not improve your state of being, just as turning up the radio to mask the sound of a car's failing engine does nothing to fix the problem—the car will run poorly and the engine will eventually fail whether or not music is playing.

Starting today, dedicate a portion of your daily routine to meditation, specifically mindful mediation, a practice of purposely bringing one's attention to the present-moment without evaluation. Start with 5-minutes a day and work up to longer periods of time when you feel comfortable. Like woking out, it is critical that you are consistent with the practice if you wish to experience noticeable results. There is a plethora of information on mindful mediation that you can find with a quick Google search, but below is a small portion of the routine to which I have become accustomed.

Find a quiet spot and sit down in a comfortable position, but not slouched. Keep your eyes open and directed just above the tip of your nose. Allow them to lose focus. Breath naturally and focus on your breath. Take time to notice the sensation in your lungs as they fill with and release air. Notice the sound of your surroundings, letting them come in and out of focus without evaluating them. Do the same with any physical sensations you might feel. When a thought comes, don't indulge in it or evaluate it—acknowledge it and let it pass.

This practice will significantly calm your mind. Those intrusive thoughts of past, future, or made up worries will no longer control your thoughts. Instead of drifting off on an exhaustive string of anxious internal ramblings, you will be able to silence the thoughts almost as soon as they appear. This does not mean you ignore your thoughts. Any reoccurring thought should be analyzed and dealt with—but once a decision about the thought has been made, one based on reason, it's time to trust yourself and let it go.

Law 11:

Don't give people permission to hurt you

No one can hurt you without your permission. Words alone are not enough for you to feel insulted, no matter the intention of the offender. For you to feel insulted, you must believe that you have been insulted. Find a rock and insult it, and what have you accomplished? If someone responds to insult like a rock, what has the abuser gained? However, if the abuser has his victim's weakness to exploit, then his efforts are worth his while. This is why it is important to place value only on what no one else but yourself can control.

If someone succeeds in offending you, know that you have given them the power to do so. Let's say someone says your shirt is ugly. It can be easy to become embarrassed at a comment like that, but why? Are you wearing the shirt for this person or for yourself? What does it matter what they think about a shirt you are wearing? Who is this person to you that their opinion should define your wardrobe or how you feel about it. Let's say someone calls you fat — well, are you fat? If you are why are you offended for something that's true? If you're not, why are you offended over something that's obviously false? If the person's intent is to hurt you, why are you hanging out with them; if the person is a stranger, why do you care about what someone you don't know has to say about you. You meet a shitload of people in your lifetime and most will have a different opinion about you — good and bad. You cannot control one person's opinion, let alone everyone's. How tiresome it is to be concerned with how others see you. Just be concerned with how you see you.

Law 12:

Live in line with nature

If you shape your life according to nature, you will never be poor, if according to people's opinions, you will never be rich. You see, natural desires are limited, but those which spring from false opinions have no where to stop. So eat until you are full, find good quality clothes to protect your body, and find a safe and comfortable spot to rest your head and call your home. But be careful not to go beyond the needs that nature has set—a roof made of wood and shingles protects one from the elements just as well as a roof made of gold. The difference is that the man who builds a roof to keep dry is satisfied when his roof works as intended, whereas the man whose needs are based on opinion is not satisfied when his roof does the job of a roof. He needs more for the sake of more, for the sake of extravagance, for the sake of status—there is no limit to his thirst. It is similar in all aspects of his life—he is not satisfied when his shoe does the job of a shoe or when his wife fills the role of a wife. He remains agitated and unfulfilled.

Law 13:

Happiness should not be the goal

Never let happiness be your goal, for happiness is not a constant. Like anger, sadness, and every other human emotion, happiness comes in small, unsustainable bursts. People who make happiness the goal of their life's effort are left disappointed and exhausted—disappointed when the source of their happiness loses its allure, and exhausted by the search to find the next thing they can latch onto in an effort to fill a void they have created. Instead, let contentedness be your goal. Be so content with your life and with living in the moment that you have no thought of happiness. When happiness does come, enjoy it, but enjoy it with the understanding that it is temporary and understand that this characteristic of non-permanence is an added part of its beauty—just as one's life is made that much more precious by their mortality.

Law 14:

Be mindful of what you value

What you value leads to how you measure your worth. Value things like expensive jewelry, fast cars, designer clothing, and status, and you will inevitably measure your worth by the very same things. The problem with valuing such things is that they don't truly belong to you. You are not your jewel-encrusted watch, you are not your car or the money in your bank account —all of which can be taken in the blink of an eye. Value yourself on the content of your character, something no one can take, which is truly your own, and you will have all the value you could desire.

Similarly, if your worth is based on money, cars, power, and status, you will value others by the same criteria. However, the price of someone's car tells you little about the content of that person's character. You will be fooled again and again if your trust or take interest in a person based on what they have and not who they are.

Law 15:

Be aware of how and why you use social media

If you use social media, be aware of how and why you use it. Don't post pictures of your butt or your abs and say that you're not looking for attention. Don't post your drama on Facebook and claim that you're not seeking attention. In fact, know that you are seeking attention whenever you post anything on social media—that's kind of its thing: *social* media. It's a world where the currency is attention paid out in "likes" and comments. Such attention can be beneficial for people building brands, businesses, or trying to spread awareness for a new product or important cause, but it does little for the person trying to achieve peace of mind. How can one cultivate a peaceful mind when the source of their happiness relies on the approval of others, some of which they've never met? The only person that needs to like your butt, abs, or trip to Hawaii is you. You're the only one who needs to think you live a cool or adventurous life. So pose and post if that is what you must, but do it with an understanding that you are seeking attention; and that you are basing a portion of your worth on what others think of you or your life.

It's also not beneficial for the person seeking peace to become overly involved with consuming social media. Many spend all their free time mindlessly scrolling through hundreds of social media posts in one sitting. They become more involved with the lives of others than they are with their own. They crave the adventure and lifestyles they see online but can't put their phone down long enough to create a style for their own life. Stop looking at someone else live their life and start living your own.

Whether you consume content or post it, challenge yourself by taking extended breaks from social media. Find another way to use your time, even if it's just sitting in your own company.

Law 16:

Be kind

Don't be rude or harsh with people unnecessarily—especially those that you encounter in passing. Everyone is someone. That's not just an old woman you're passing at the store, it's someone's grandma; that's not just an old man getting gas at the pump next to you, it's someone's dad; that girl behind the counter at the store is someone's daughter; and that homeless man on the street is someone's son. Treat people with the same patience, respect, and courtesy that you would want others to treat your mom or dad with. If your mom and dad were shit, then pick someone in your life that wasn't and treat others with the respect you would want that person to be treated with.

Kindness cultivates a peaceful mind. It takes little effort to be kind to others, while the opposite is true with being mad, annoyed, or irritated. The former allows you to go about your day unhindered, while the latter requires that you entrust your peace of mind to everyone, letting them live rent-free in your head until your emotions subside.

Know that being kind does not mean being a pushover. The two have no connection.

Law 17:

Be a person you can trust

Live in such a way that your future self can trust your former self, and that your present self can trust your future self. Many anxieties arise from either worrying about how one has acted in the past or how one will act in the future—instead, be concerned with how you are acting now. The more you act in line with your principles and trust reason to determine what is best, the less anxious you will be about your past actions. As for the future, take comfort in knowing that you will come to it armed with the same reasoning that you possess now.

Law 18:

Check yourself

Make a habit of reflecting on your day. Where did things go well, where did they go wrong, what lessons did you learn, and how will you implement those lessons? If you want to grow as a person, you need to know in which areas you need growth. Just as a garden left unattended will fill with weeds and pests, an unchecked life will cultivate weeds and pests of its own.

The same goes for disagreements. Understand that no one is right all the time. If you walk away from every dispute thinking you have come out victorious or that your position was the correct one—it's likely that you haven't checked yourself.

Law 19:

Be grateful

The mind is quickly aware of things that go wrong but overlooks all that which is going well. As a result, people place more value on things they don't have than on the things they do have and are more upset when things go wrong than they are appreciative when things go right. Who do you think will have a better day, the person who is upset that it's raining or the person who is grateful for their umbrella? Actively seek out things you are grateful for — the warmth from the sun, the sight of a friend, a cold breeze on a warm day, or having an umbrella on a rainy day. It sounds simple, but practicing this will change your life.

Law 20:

There will be good times and there will be bad times

The only constant thing in life is change. Nothing lasts forever, be it good times or bad times. Every ripe fruit rots, every fire dies out, every joy subsides, and every emotion we hold eventually fades, giving way to new feelings. Don't let yourself be deceived by the gifts of fortune, no matter how great the gift. In fact, be more cautious the more desirable the gift. Enjoy it while you have it, but prepare your mind with the thought that these gifts of fortune can and one day will disappear as suddenly as they arrive. Understand, too, that when that time comes, you would be foolish to be upset or mad that they are gone, just as you would be foolish to be upset that they were given to you in the first place. The giving and returning of such gifts are out of your control. You should not agonize over such things any more than you should be upset that the sun sets or rises. Such things are a part of nature.

Take comfort in this understanding of change. Appreciate the good times that much more with the knowledge that they will not last forever, and find the same solace in the fact that the bad times, too, will eventually end. Enjoy the moment, but don't be foolish and expect that moment to last forever, and don't be even more foolish by becoming anxious that it will end.

Accept that such things are out of your control. It does not matter how much you cry, for fortune feels no sympathy.

Law 21:

Live in a way that will make your past and future self proud

What do you wish you did yesterday? How do you wish you would have acted? Did you make a promise to yourself that you didn't keep? Did you pass on the opportunity to complete work you had been putting off? Most of us have a long list of promises we have yet to keep. We leave them for tomorrow as if our "future selves" will be more qualified or more willing to complete them. But the only way your future self will be the person you want them to be is by becoming that person today. If you're serious about living a better, more peaceful life, the work starts today—this instant. In every action, emotion, or reaction, make a habit of asking yourself, "How would I react to this if I was the person I wanted to be? How would that person handle this situation?" You don't have to be perfect in your attempts to be that version of yourself, but you need to make the attempt. And if you're not yet making the attempt, you must, at the very least, realize that you need to make the attempt. Otherwise, you're destined to live a life where you're forever a day away from becoming the person you want to be.

Law 22:

Confront your anxieties with reason

Don't run from your anxieties and don't hide from them by distracting your mind with media, drugs, or alcohol. You must come to realize that it is impossible to escape your anxieties by hiding from them, because it is you who create them. Instead, you must confront them head-on. Analyze them with reason, asking, "Is this thing, which twists my stomach and causes me to pull out my hair, something that I can control, or is it something that is outside of my power." And if it's something out of your control, drop it from your list of concerns—for it is pointless to give energy to something which you have no power over. Don't cry that it's raining, grab an umbrella; don't whine that your nose is running, wipe it.

Of course, this is easier said than done. Some of us have anxieties that are born out of a complex history of adversity. They stem from years of mental, and even physical abuse. They are created through an upbringing in which we had no say, and are strengthened by a mental state created in an effort to protect itself. Confronting these deeper anxieties, which most of us face on some level, will require consistent work. It will require you to look back and analyze past experiences, to question why you carry yourself the way you do, to find lessons in tragedy, to accept that the past is no longer in your control and that you hold no definite sway on the future, for even tomorrow is not guaranteed. The work will be hard, but the solution is always the same—do not merely distract yourself from your anxieties, confront them with reason.

Law 23:

Don't worry about what other people have

Do not be concerned with what other people have. Do not use their lives to judge the value of yours. And don't be fooled and judge the quality of their life based on the quality of their car, house, or other material possessions. You can hate yourself while sailing on a yacht and love yourself while riding public transit. *Things* do not make a man whole. *Things* do not offer everlasting peace. *Things* only lead to the wanting for more things. "A new car will make me happy," ok, you get a new car, now what? "An expensive bag will make me happy," you buy the bag, now what? People tend to think that once they obtain the thing they want, they will be forever happy and content. They confuse momentary excitement for the possibility of everlasting peace. They base their happiness, their worth, and the value of their lives on something unstable and unsustainable. This only leads to jealousy, envy, and frustration. Learn to value what is truly your own—your character—and you will never feel the urge to look in your neighbor's yard for what you don't have.

Law: 24

You are not responsible for other people's feelings

Whether you love them or hate them, you are not responsible for other people's feelings. They, like you, are responsible for their own opinions which dictate their feelings. Still, if a loved one is hurt, sad, or depressed, try to understand their position and, if possible, help them find a resolution or be a shoulder for them to lean on until they do. But do not let their feelings overtake you, especially if they cannot be resolved. Know that to persist in being sad, angry, or depressed because someone you love is hurt, does nothing to resolve their pain.

On the other hand, if they believe that you are the cause of their hurt, while you are not responsible for their feelings, you *are* responsible for your intentions. So make sure that you are always acting with the best of intentions. If your intentions are misunderstood, communicate them with that person in an effort to clear the air and come to a better understanding.

.

Law 25:

Become ok with rejection and embarrassment

In regards to obtaining something you think will better you or provide you with a more peaceful life— nothing is worse than not trying. Embarrassment, fear of failure, or rejection are poor excuses for not applying for a dream job, starting a new venture, building a new relationship, or making a new friend. Embarrassment and fear are like any other emotion: manageable and temporary. And like most negative emotions, if we can identify their root cause, we can eradicate them. We would do better to face these emotions than attempt to hide from them. The more you face them, the more comfortable you will become with them and the less power they will have over you. With the right mindset, you can escape embarrassment altogether.

Law 26:

Every mistake contains a lesson

There is a lesson to be learned from every mistake you make, even the worst ones. Realizing this is the key to living a content life. Many are quick to let the feelings that come with a mistake infect their spirit. They allow it to fester, growing until the remorse becomes a larger issue than the mistake itself. Whatever the situation—a failed relationship, a missed opportunity, a lapse in character—there is a lesson to be found. Let finding, learning, and applying that lesson be the end of your remorse! Do not let your mistakes define you. Define yourself by how you respond to your mistakes, how you shape a lesson out of every seemingly unfortunate circumstance—because for you, every mistake is fortunate. Every mistake uncovers a chink in your armor in need of repair, which may have never been brought to your attention otherwise.

Law 27:

Know what you control and what you do not

It does nothing to concern yourself with what you can't control. Many people would love to have the power of flight, but no one is crying themselves to sleep because they weren't born with wings. We accept it as a part of nature, and while we would like to be able to fly by our own power, we don't hold it against ourselves or god that we can't. We should adopt a similar attitude with all things we don't control. The next time you are bothered by something, ask yourself, "Is this something I can or cannot control?" If it's something you can't control, let it go. To continue to be bothered by something you have no power over is as silly as crying because you weren't born with wings. Still, do what you can do about the thing that's bothering you, but know and accept your limits. In the case of flight, we may not have the ability to soar by our own power, but through the understanding of human limitations and the power of innovation, man has created multiple vehicles in which humans can take flight.

Law 28:

Healthy conversations are not about winning

If you find yourself trying to win an argument with a loved one, stop and reassess your goal.

Law 29:

Keep the promises you make to yourself

The only way you can learn to trust yourself is to keep the promises you make to yourself. Treat yourself with some respect—how can you expect anyone to respect you if you don't respect yourself? Take more time and consideration before making promises to yourself. Make sure that they are worth your time and effort before committing. Stop neglecting your relationship with yourself.

Law 30:

Do not lie

Work to be a person that doesn't need to lie — even if it is a white lie. Lying creates more lies. It destroys trust and slowly chips away at relationships with others and yourself, even white lies. If you feel the need to lie, find out why. If you're doing something that you shouldn't be doing, don't do that thing. If you are trying to spare someone's feelings, don't. Most people would rather be spoken to plainly than manipulated with words. It's too much shit to keep track of anyway. Lying inherently leads to a more chaotic life.

Law 31:

Work towards being a friend to yourself

Give yourself the same respect you give others. We are quick to hand out words of encouragement to our friends and family but feel we are unworthy of the same treatment from ourselves. Learn to be a friend to yourself and learn to love yourself. If you think you are a person unworthy of self-love, then work to be a person who deserves it and love yourself for that.

Law 32:

Be comfortable in your own company

If you're not comfortable in your own company and find yourself having to find distraction in music, podcasts, or TV anytime you are alone, you need to find out what it is about yourself that you are uncomfortable with and work to fix it. Many people don't like to be alone with their thoughts, some to the extent that they must consume some type of media as they drift off to sleep. But these distractions do not solve the underlying issue. If you're not comfortable being alone with your thoughts, you must identify why and work to fix it. We should all be able to bear an extended period of time alone with ourselves without distractions. You should be able to sit with yourself as if you were sitting with a friend.

Law 33:

Do not see events as good or bad

No one is to blame for your misfortune. And it is only misfortune because you have labeled it as such. Other men have been through the same events, but instead of misfortune, they have labeled it opportunity. Who will lead a more peaceful life, the man who sees every dilemma as a personal slight, a misfortune that was unfair and unavoidable, or the man that sees the same situation as an opportunity for growth, a sign to pivot? You have no control over the events of life, but you do control how you react to them. And how you react to such events will inevitably make you. So stop saying something was "bad" or "good," only your reactions to such events should be labeled "bad" or "good."

Law 34:

Assess what is important to you

Take time to seriously consider what it is you deem important in this life and whether or not those things should be placed at such a high value. Be sure they are sustainable and controlled only by you. Otherwise, you will be controlled by whoever possesses them.

Law 35:

Do not follow blindly

Do not blindly follow someone just because they are praised by others. Do not trust the words of a philosopher because they are well-known or come from ancient times. Similarly, do not dislike someone just because they are looked down upon by the masses. In every matter of life, do your own research when possible. Don't just read this book and say, "well, these are the laws for a peaceful life. They're in a book, so it must be true." No, hold them under a microscope, test them, prove them, and, if you can, improve them.

Law 36:

Be comfortable being uncomfortable

Get comfortable being uncomfortable, for this is the fire where the most rewarding things in life are forged. True character is formed during uncomfortable times, and some of the most significant opportunities lie at the center of uncomfortable situations. Every great accomplishment requires a person to, at one time or another, be uncomfortable. Olympic athletes have their comfort torn away during training so that they may prepare their bodies for upcoming challenges. Entrepreneurs often give up everything for a chance to pursue a venture only they feel is worthy. Mothers give up comfort to bring children into the world; fathers put aside their comfort to provide for their families. Every great and worthy thing requires one to let go of some portion of their comfort. Even the man fighting temptation gives up the comfort of his former ways so that he may grow.

Law 37:

Try your best not to make assumptions

Yes, there are situations where making assumptions is necessary, such as when deciding the safest street to walk down at night or when encountering a stray dog. However, in most scenarios where your life is not in threat of any danger, assuming creates more problems than it solves—specifically in conversation. Before making assumptions, ask directly for the information you're trying to obtain. If that information is purposely withheld from you, then you may have no other option than to assume based on the information you possess. Of course, how you should react will depend on the scenario. But, as a general rule, try not to assume. In most cases, it does nothing but make an ass out of you and the other person. "To assume makes an ass out of you and me (ass-u-me)."

Law 38:

A good life does not require praise

Nothing of true worth gets its quality from praise. The structural quality of a house is not determined by praise, and the strength of a wall isn't determined by how many people applaud its creation— the same goes for life. The quality of life is not dependent on how many people approve and praise your path any more than the quality of a roof is based on the words spoken about it. A good life does not require praise from others.

Law 39:

The true man is revealed in difficult times

True character is created in difficult times. When life gets tough and you feel your character start to falter, that is when sticking to your principles matters most. It's easy to be the best version of yourself in good times, just as it is easier to avoid temptations when they are out of reach, but much harder when they are placed before you. Next time life gets tough, see it as a test, an opportunity to prove the quality of your character.

Law 40:

Don't be afraid of change

Change comes in many forms: death, tragedy, loss, exile, birth, love, and hate. Do not fear change, in any of its forms, or be anxious of its arrival. Change is a necessary part of nature and is just as important to the whole as it is to the individual. Nothing could exist without change—the butterfly cannot come to be without the caterpillar, food does not exist without death (be that of an animal or plant), and a boy cannot become a man without change. In short, there is no growth without change!

Law 41:

Be consistent

The secret to any sustainable success is consistency. Try hard to remember this — it is the key to accomplishing your goals. The person who practices the piano for ten minutes every day will be better than the person who practices piano sporadically and only when they're feeling up to it.

Consistency is an obvious necessity when you're talking about learning to play an instrument, but the need for consistency should be just as apparent in every aspect of your life. Living a good life requires consistency; living your principles requires consistency; maintaining a relationship with yourself and others requires consistency, living in peace requires consistency. Your goals can't be something you work towards only when you're feeling up to it.

Law 42:

Don't be a people-pleaser

Do not be a person who bends over backwards in an effort to please someone. Understand that if someone is not pleased, it is from their own doing and can only be undone by their own doing. There are some people who will do anything to avoid conflict, even if it means changing their entire personality to please another person. There is nothing wrong with conforming yourself to specific situations—everyone who has ever worked a customer service job understands the importance of this ability—but if you are changing who you are in an effort to receive validation from others, you are on a bad path. Do not base your worth on how happy you can make someone else, and do not look outside yourself for validation.

But understand that there is a difference between being a people-pleaser and being thoughtful. If your grandma is cold, get her a blanket; if your girlfriend is sick, do what you can to comfort her; and in an argument, it is ok to find a compromise. It's ok to consider the feelings of others and, at times, approach someone with more compassion because of what they might be going through.

Law 43:

Don't put things off

If you can do it now, do it now. Don't start eating better tomorrow, do it now. Don't start exercising tomorrow, start today. Don't put off taking out the trash or cleaning your room, do it now. There is no need or benefit in putting things off. Most of the time, we trick ourselves into believing that we need to wait — some say they need time to mentally prepare, others say they need to relax beforehand, and many more will make up some other bullshit excuse. If you have the time to do it, do it now (even if you only have time to finish a portion of the overall task). If you find yourself arguing with yourself to start whatever task is at hand, count to five, and without thinking, as soon as you say "five," get up and start. A majority of the time, as soon as you start the task you will wonder why you were so reluctant to start it in the first place.

Law 44:

Feeling good is good enough

Once you go beyond practicality, there is no end. If you want peace of mind, self-assurance, and a content life, then understand that feeling good is good enough— beyond that is nothing but a desire that can not be satisfied. If you buy shoes to protect your feet, your needs are met once the foot is protected. If you buy shoes for the sole purpose of style, you'll never be satisfied and end up dying surrounded by 100 pairs of Jordans. There is nothing wrong with wanting the newest pair of shoes or the most trendy gear—however, it is an endless pursuit. You could already be satisfied, but instead, give up time and money to buy a glimpse of satisfaction that escapes you almost as fast as it arrived.

Law 44:

Move Silently

No one needs to know your every move, especially those in development; let your results speak for themselves. Remember this, especially when someone tells you about their own achievements or ventures. It can be tempting to respond in kind but don't. In most cases, there is no point in telling someone what you're *going to do,* other than to stroke your ego. Instead, just do it.

Of course, in certain cases, it is healthy to tell your loved ones what you're up to, both for them and you. So, if you're going to tell someone about your personal matters, make sure it's someone you love and trust. But be careful because, for some, revealing one's plans before they are accomplished can trick the brain into no longer feeling the need to accomplish the goal.

Law 44:

Embrace the grind

Life gets hard, don't run from it, embrace it. Know that both the coward and the hero feel the same: both are scared and nervous. However, the coward lets his nerves get the best of him, whereas the hero embraces and overcomes them. To that end, be the person who embraces the ugly and the miserable. Be the person who embraces hard work and the grind. Don't be afraid of getting hurt or sacrificing some blood. This is your life; live every moment of it.

Law 44:

Do not be afraid to be wrong

If someone can show you your mistake in any thought or action, gladly change. Let your goal be to seek the truth, which you shouldn't let harm you. The harm is to continue in one's own self-deception and ignorance.

Here are several ways you can use the following pages:

1. Reflect on what you are grateful for

2. Write down your goals for the day

3. Reflect on how you need to improve **today** in order to be a person you are proud of

4. Reflect on your progress of the day

5. Reflect on mistakes of the day and derive lessons from them

6. Reflect on words from the book

7. Prepare for the day: what difficulties might you encounter? How will you face them?

8. Reflect on your day: What did I do? Where did I go wrong? Where did I go right? Was there anything I left undone?

9. Answer the provided question on each page.

What type of person do you want to be?

What are you good at?

In what areas of life do you need improvement?

What is your most reoccurring worry?

When do you feel most at ease?

What is your definition of a success?

What type of friend do you want to be?

What upcoming changes are you most afraid of?

Do you trust yourself? Why or why not?

Are you proud of yourself? Why or why not?

What could you have done better today?

.

When was the last time you disappointed yourself?

What advice would you give to someone who is trying to live a good life?

What do you want most in life?

What do you value the most in life?

How much time do you waste on things you dislike?
What are they?

What is something that you are putting off? Why?

Are you the best version of yourself?

What does the best version of yourself look like?

What is the most important thing in your life?

Do you love yourself?

If you had one year left to live, how would you spend it?

If you had one week left to live, how would you spend it?

If you had one day left to live, how would you spend it?

What advice would you give your younger self?

Is there something you're still holding on to? Is it time to let it go?

What's the last mistake you made and what lesson can you take from it?

What goals do you want to accomplish by the end of the year?

What is holding you back from being the best version of yourself?

What is your top priority in life right now?

What is the biggest thing you can do now that will change your life for the better?

Do you love your life? Explain.

Do you like your job? Explain.

What does your ideal life look like?

Is there anything you are running away from or avoiding?

What good habits do you want to cultivate?

What bad habits do you want to break?

Are you living your life to the fullest? If not, what is stopping you?

How can you make your life more meaningful, starting today?

What type of qualities do you want to embody?

Who are the most important people to you?

Do you appreciate your loved ones enough?

How will your life be different in a year?

What are you grateful for?

What nice thing can you do for someone else today?

How much do you worry about what others think?

Made in the USA
Columbia, SC
30 July 2024